THREATS TO CIVIL LIBERTIES

Threats to Civil Liberties: SPEECH

Stephen Currie

San Diego, CA

For more information, contact:
ReferencePoint Press, Inc.
PO Box 27779
San Diego, CA 92198
www.ReferencePointPress.com

LIBRARY OF CONGRESS CATALOGING-IN-PUBLICATION DATA

Name: Currie, Stephen, author.
Title: Threats to Civil Liberties: Speech/by Stephen Currie.
Description: San Diego, CA: ReferencePoint Press, Inc., [2019] | Series: Threats to Civil Liberties | Includes bibliographical references and index.
Identifiers: | ISBN 9781682824566 (eBook) | ISBN 9781682824559 (hardback)
Subjects: LCSH: Free speech—United States—Juvenile literature. | Civil rights—United States—Juvenile literature.

CONTENTS

Free Speech

The right to speak freely is one of the basic principles of American life. With few exceptions, people in the United States can speak freely without fearing that the government will punish them for their words. In general, protection extends even to speech that is unpopular or offensive. Americans may use harsh words to criticize their government, speak in favor of political ideas despised by most of the country, and use insulting language toward their neighbors and strangers alike—and still expect that they will not be penalized by government officials. The ability to speak freely is treasured by many, if not most, Americans. "The right to free speech is as powerful as sword and shield," says writer Laurel Lancaster. "I consistently remind myself what a privilege it is to speak and write as I see fit, without fear of retribution."[1]

Freedom of speech is established in the US Constitution. Specifically, it appears in the First Amendment to the Constitution, part of a set of ten amendments, or additions to the original document, known as the Bill of Rights. The First Amendment guarantees several freedoms: freedom of religion, freedom of the press, freedom to assemble, freedom to petition government for change, and perhaps most importantly, freedom of speech. "Congress," the amendment declares, "shall make no law . . . abridging the freedom of speech."[2] Writing and publishing a book, giving a speech, posting messages online, even drawing a cartoon for a magazine—the First Amendment says that these are all legal acts, except in a handful of specific situations, and the government may not pass laws criminalizing any of them.

Defining and Protecting Speech

The United States was one of the first nations anywhere to guarantee freedom of speech. Today, though many other countries have established freedom of speech as well, the United States still goes beyond most others where speech rights are concerned. Even countries that are largely free and democratic often criminalize speech that in the United States is entirely legal. Germany, for example, makes it a crime to deny that the Holocaust of World War II ever took place; the United States does not. Ireland bans blasphemy, or the mocking of a deity or a religion; blasphemy is not a crime in the United States. South Korea sharply limits the ability of citizens to spread negative information about political candidates; no US law does the same. The United States stands out in the degree to which it protects the speech of its people.

> "The right to free speech is as powerful as sword and shield."[1]
>
> —Writer Laurel Lancaster

In the United States, moreover, the definition of speech is exceptionally broad. As the word suggests, *speech* includes everything that people say: formal lectures, casual conversation, and so on. It also includes writings: books, magazine articles, message board posts, and advertisements, among others. Freedom of speech covers the visual arts—painting, photography, sculpture—and music. Under the First Amendment, therefore, authors cannot generally be prosecuted for the books they write, political candidates cannot be jailed for the speeches they give, and painters and cartoonists cannot be arrested for the images they produce. Even if these works are offensive or unpopular, their creators are—at least in theory—safe from being penalized by the government.

> "Congress shall make no law . . . abridging the freedom of speech."[2]
>
> —First Amendment to the US Constitution

What constitutes speech goes further, however. Freedom of speech includes the right not to speak at all—a right sometimes

Women participate in the Women's March in San Francisco in 2018. People in the United States can speak freely and protest peacefully without fearing government punishment.

exercised by students who prefer not to say the Pledge of Allegiance at school. Displaying a flag, American or otherwise, is a form of speech, and judges have ruled that burning a flag is speech too. Speech includes contributions to political campaigns. Some courts—though not all—have ruled that even exotic dancing is a type of speech. Freedom of speech, then, does not simply mean the freedom to teach a class, have a conversation, or write an article. Freedom of speech covers a wide variety of actions beyond the speaking or writing of words—and all of these actions are protected.

Attacks on Free Speech

Though the constitutional commitment to freedom of speech in the United States is quite strong, throughout history the free-speech rights of Americans have frequently been under attack. In 1798, less than a decade after the ratification of the Constitution, President John Adams signed a bill making criticism of the federal government and its officials illegal. Under this law a writer named James Callender served a prison term, for example, for publishing his opinion that Adams was a "repulsive pedant, a gross hypocrite and an unprincipled oppressor."[3] During the Civil War people could be arrested in the North for singing Confederate songs. Woodrow Wilson, who was president during World War I, criminalized the distribution of leaflets that opposed the war, and the US Supreme Court agreed with his decision. "When a nation is at war," the court ruled, "many things that might be said in time of peace are such a hindrance to its effort that their utterance will not be endured so long as men fight."[4]

The threats to free speech continue today. Sometimes the threats come from college administrators or university students. In 2017 the mayor of Jerusalem, Israel, was scheduled to speak at San Francisco State University in California, but the event ended abruptly when a group of protesters, convinced that the mayor did not respect the rights of Palestinians, disrupted the proceedings. Threats can also come from the media. In 2017 television commentator Lou Dobbs, furious that Barack Obama had criticized Donald Trump, called for Obama's arrest. "He should be brought back by the marshals," Dobbs said. "Isn't there some law that says presidents shouldn't be attacking sitting presidents?"[5] As it happens, even former presidents have the right to speak freely. But threats to free-speech rights can come from almost anywhere. How best to deal with attacks on free speech is one of the great civil rights questions of today.

CHAPTER 1

Unprotected Speech

Free speech in the United States has traditionally been interpreted broadly. That is, most judges and legal scholars start from the assumption that people generally have the right to express themselves freely without government interference. Courts therefore are usually reluctant to interfere with a person's right to speak unless they see a compelling reason to limit that right. This perspective has led to official acceptance of many types of speech that might well be banned in some other countries. In the United States, for example, political groups considered dangerous by government police agencies may march openly, crude language is widely permitted, and even some speech that advocates violence is tolerated.

But although freedom of speech covers a wide variety of situations, it is not absolute. On the contrary, there are several scenarios in which courts have ruled that the right to free speech is outweighed by other considerations. Still other restrictions on speech come not from governments but from private employers or organizations, which are not subject to the First Amendment in the same way as the government. Not all speech, then, is protected. To understand how the concept of freedom of speech is under attack in the United States today, it is instructive to examine the situations in which free speech does not apply.

Defamation

One such situation involves defamation of character—the deliberate spreading of lies about someone else in an attempt to humiliate, ridicule, or damage that person's reputation. When defamation takes the form of speech, it is typically known as slander. When it is done in print, it is usually called libel. The reason for excluding libel and slander from speech protection is straightforward: While free speech is important, so too is the principle that, as a legal encyclopedia puts it, "people should not ruin others' lives by telling lies about them."[6] American leaders have weighed the advantages of free speech against the drawbacks caused by doing harm to others and determined that the right to free speech should not make it possible to spread malicious lies.

> "People should not ruin others' lives by telling lies about them."[6]
>
> —Emily Doskow, author of a legal reference book

It is important to note that in the United States, defamation is not a criminal act. The police will not arrest a person who carries out libel or slander, government prosecutors will not try a case against the defamer, and the defamer will not be imprisoned. However, though defamation is not a crime, it is a tort, meaning that the person being defamed may sue for damages in civil court. Through a privately hired attorney, the victim will then try to convince a judge or jury that defamation took place. If the case is decided in favor of the victim, the defamer may be forced to pay the victim monetary damages. The money may help make up for the damage done to the victim's life, especially if the lies have resulted in the victim's being unjustly fired, evicted from housing, or otherwise suffering because of the lies.

While it is possible to win a defamation case, the bar is set high. Simply criticizing a person is not enough to establish defamation, even if the criticism is harsh. First, any defamatory statement must be framed as a fact. Opinions, however viciously expressed, do not qualify. Second, defamation must be provably false. Truth is a defense against libel and slander; a claim that a government official is corrupt is not defamation if the official is indeed accepting bribes or taking kickbacks. Third, the speaker must know that the criticism is untrue, or at least make the statement without caring whether the words are true or false. A person who spreads untruthful statements about others while believing that they are accurate will generally not owe damages.

Fourth, the statement must cause actual harm to the person being defamed. That can be financial harm, as in the case of a person who loses a job due to unfounded allegations, or it can be harm to a person's reputation. In either situation, though, it must be evident that the person has suffered in some way because of the defamation. Fifth, defamatory statements must be public. Even a knowingly false claim is not defamatory if it is contained only within a private e-mail or spoken as part of a personal conversation. And finally, many states allow publications such as newspapers to escape libel charges if they print a retraction, or a statement admitting that the original story was false.

At a 2017 rally in Tennessee, white supremacists form a wall of shields to lock out anyone who was not a member of the hate group. Even groups considered dangerous by government agencies are allowed to speak freely and march openly.

For all these reasons, successful defamation suits are relatively rare. Lawyers are often reluctant to take defamation cases because there are many different possible lines of defense. The person who made the statement can argue that it was only an opinion, that he or she did not know the statement was untrue, or that the statement caused no actual harm to the complainant. In particular, celebrities rarely sue tabloids that make up outright lies about them. Rather than draw further attention to the claims made in the articles, celebrities often decide it is better to ignore the statements and hope readers do not believe them.

Successful Defamation Suits

But when defamation cases can be brought, judges and juries typically take them very seriously. In 2016, for example, North Carolina state employee Beth Desmond sued a newspaper, the *Raleigh News & Observer*, and Mandy Locke, one of the newspaper's reporters. Desmond had testified for the government as a firearms analyst in a high-profile murder trial. The defendant in the case was ultimately found guilty, based in part on the evidence provided by Desmond. Following the trial, however, the *News and Observer* printed several articles by Locke questioning the guilty verdict in the case. The articles quoted firearms experts who seemed to suggest that Desmond had manufactured evidence to help the prosecution make its case.

The negative coverage had an immediate impact on Desmond's life and career. The articles, she asserted later on, had given her post-traumatic stress disorder and made prosecutors and defense attorneys unwilling to hire her to testify in trials. When four of Locke's sources complained that the articles had either misquoted them or taken their statements out of context, Desmond sued both Locke and the newspaper for damages. Desmond claimed that the articles had gone to print even though the reporter knew that the allegations were false. "They have a power," Desmond's lawyer told the jury, referring to the newspaper's publishers. "With the flick of a pen they can wreak havoc on somebody's life."[7] The jury agreed and awarded Desmond a multimillion-dollar verdict.

Even a few celebrities have successfully sued for damages when they believed an article was too outrageous or damaging to ignore. The most famous of these took place in 1976, when a tabloid called the *National Enquirer* claimed that comedian Carol Burnett was drunk at a restaurant in Washington, DC. Burnett, who had long been known for her activism against alcoholism, was incensed. She knew she had not been drunk on the night in question, and she was convinced that the article made her out to be a hypocrite. She sued the tabloid and was able to demonstrate that the *National Enquirer* had made the story up. Burnett subsequently won her case, eventually collecting an estimated $200,000 in damages.

> **"With the flick of a pen they can wreak havoc on somebody's life."[7]**
>
> —The lawyer for a government employee suing a newspaper reporter and publisher for libel

Inciting Illegal Activity

A second exemption from free-speech laws involves speech that in the opinion of government agents is "directed to inciting or producing imminent lawless action and is likely to incite or produce such action."[8] The phrase "imminent lawless action" generally implies that speech can be banned if it simultaneously does three things. First, it must have the effect of encouraging those who hear or read it to break the law. Second, it must encourage those people to engage in illegal activity right away. And third, the breaking of laws must be a probable outcome of the speech. A speaker at a rally who tells listeners to immediately start shooting police officers, for example, would almost certainly be violating the standard. In contrast, a person who publishes a magazine article arguing that violent revolution against the government might someday be necessary probably would not.

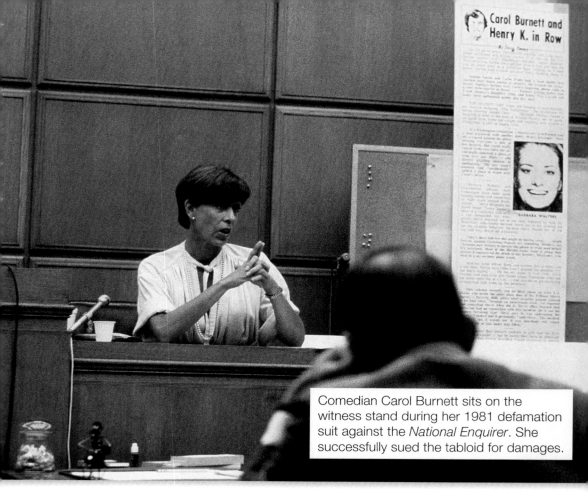

Comedian Carol Burnett sits on the witness stand during her 1981 defamation suit against the *National Enquirer*. She successfully sued the tabloid for damages.

The "imminent lawless action" standard is designed to be difficult to meet. Judges frequently rule in favor of defendants who are charged with inciting criminal behavior, even when the activity in question is clearly against the law. In a famous 1969 case known as *Brandenburg v. Ohio*, for example, Ku Klux Klan leader Clarence Brandenburg gave a speech urging his listeners to take "revengeance"[9] against African Americans and Jews. Such advocacy broke an Ohio state law against encouraging violence, and Brandenburg was arrested, tried, and convicted. The US Supreme Court, however, threw out the conviction. The justices believed that the Ohio law was too broad. Brandenburg was certainly advocating violence, but there was no indication that he meant his followers to engage in it right away. Thus, his words were protected as free speech.

The First Amendment Protects Burning the American Flag

The 1989 case *Texas v. Johnson* involved Gregory Johnson's arrest for burning a US flag as part of a protest. The Supreme Court determined that flag-burning, as a form of speech, was protected under the First Amendment. Justice William Brennan wrote:

> We can imagine no more appropriate response to burning a flag than waving one's own, no better way to counter a flag burner's message than by saluting the flag that burns. . . . We do not consecrate the flag by punishing its desecration, for in doing so we dilute the freedom that this cherished emblem represents. Johnson was convicted for engaging in expressive conduct. The State's interest in preventing breaches of the peace does not support his conviction, because Johnson's conduct did not threaten to disturb the peace. Nor does the State's interest in preserving the flag as a symbol of nationhood and national unity justify his criminal conviction for engaging in political expression.

Quoted in Justia, "*Texas v. Johnson*, 491 U.S. 397 (1989)." https://supreme.justia.com.

A few cases, however, have been decided in the other direction. Among the most famous of these was a 1997 case known as *Rice v. Paladin Enterprises*. Paladin Enterprises was a publishing company. In 1983 it printed a book called *Hit Man: A Technical Manual for Independent Contractors*. In essence, *Hit Man* was an instruction book for people who wanted to learn how to commit murder for hire. Ten years after the book's publication, Maryland resident Lawrence Horn hired a criminal named James Perry to kill three people, including Horn's son and ex-wife. Perry carried out the murders but soon afterward was arrested for the crimes.

At the trial, it developed that Perry had used information from *Hit Man* to help him plan the killings. Members of the victims' fami-

The First Amendment Does Not Protect Burning the American Flag

Not all Supreme Court justices agreed with Brennan. Three justices dissented, arguing that the flag was too important a symbol of national unity, so destroying one should not be protected speech. As Chief Justice William Rehnquist put it:

> The American flag, then, throughout more than 200 years of our history, has come to be the visible symbol embodying our Nation. It does not represent the views of any particular political party, and it does not represent any particular political philosophy. The flag is not simply another "idea" or "point of view" competing for recognition in the marketplace of ideas. Millions and millions of Americans regard it with an almost mystical reverence. . . . I cannot agree that the First Amendment invalidates the Act of Congress, and the laws of 48 of the 50 States, which make criminal the public burning of the flag.

Quoted in Justia, "*Texas v. Johnson*, 491 U.S. 397 (1989)." https://supreme.justia.com.

lies filed a civil suit against Paladin, arguing that the words of the book represented an incitement to violence. They argued that the sole purpose of the book was to help readers commit crimes. A federal court eventually agreed with the families. As the unanimous decision put it, "Perry followed, in painstaking detail, countless of the book's instructions in soliciting, preparing for, and carrying out his murders."[10] Free speech, the court ruled, did not extend to writing a how-to manual for contract killers.

Malicious Harassment

The imminent lawless action standard deals with situations in which a speaker incites others to engage in illegal activity, especially in violence. But speakers and writers who issue threats of their own may not be covered by free-speech protections either. No one has the right to threaten to kill another person, for example. Nor is it acceptable to threaten to injure someone else. In the United States threats such as these often fall into a category called malicious harassment, and malicious harassment is a crime.

As is true of inciting violence in others, the criteria for what constitutes malicious harassment can be quite strict. To qualify as malicious harassment, for instance, speech must actually promise violence. A person who swears at someone else or calls another person offensive names will not typically be charged with a crime. In the same way, there needs to be a good chance that the threat will be carried out. A threat that is clearly made in jest, for instance, probably qualifies for free-speech protections, while more serious threats will not. "If you walk into a store with a gun and threaten to shoot the clerk unless she gives you a refund," points out legal expert Mark Theoharis, "such a threat is credible and specific."[11] In this example, free-speech protections will likely not apply.

> "If you walk into a store with a gun and threaten to shoot the clerk unless she gives you a refund, such a threat is credible and specific."[11]
>
> —Legal expert Mark Theoharis

Indeed, threats of violence against individual people are often taken seriously by police forces and other law enforcement agencies. This is especially true where public figures are concerned. In 2007, for example, a student in Indiana posted messages online calling for the assassination of then-president George W. Bush and urging the rape and murder of Bush's wife. The student was charged, tried, and sentenced to prison. In 2010 a Texas man was likewise arrested, tried, and imprisoned for advocating the death of then-president Barack Obama. "People, the time has come for revolution," he wrote. "It is time for Obama to die."[12] These threats were ruled to be legitimate, specific, and serious, and so they were not subject to the protections of the First Amendment.

As in many free-speech situations, however, the line between protected speech and unprotected speech can vary where threats are concerned. In 2008, for example, California resident Walter Bagdasarian wrote online messages threatening the life of Obama, then a candidate for president. Bagdasarian was arrested and convicted, but his lawyers appealed the verdict. They argued that Bagdasarian had no intention of carrying out an assassination, noting that Bagdasarian had posted under a pseudonym and that only a few people who read the post took it seriously enough to report it. The appeals court agreed and overturned the conviction. Nonetheless, as the Indiana and Texas cases make clear, people who make legitimate threats against others should not generally expect to be protected under free-speech laws.

Obscenity

As with defamation and threats of violence, First Amendment protections have traditionally not been extended to obscenity—that is, speech that has the power to disgust listeners or readers. This category most often includes pornographic videos and images but has been applied to texts as well. Many court cases have been brought in the past half century alleging that certain books, films, or other materials are obscene and that the government has every right to prevent their publication or distribution. But few of these cases are decided against the people making or distributing the materials, mainly because there is no consistent definition of obscenity and no consensus about what it actually encompasses.

Without an objective standard, judges have resorted to subjective ones. Supreme Court justice Potter Stewart once said, "I know [obscenity] when I see it."[13] But that is a poor legal guideline, especially given that Stewart died in 1985. Prosecutors have generally concluded that courts will rule against them in obscenity cases, and so prosecutions of this type have become

First Amendment protections have traditionally not been extended to obscenity, which usually includes pornography. This is because there is no consistent definition of what obscenity encompasses.

rare. Federal courts today hear only a handful of cases each year in which depiction of adult sexual behavior is an issue, although Attorney General Jeff Sessions, who took office in 2017, says he plans to try more cases of this type.

One category of obscene speech does remain of great interest to law enforcement, however. That is child pornography. Police forces work hard to stamp out images and written descriptions of children involved in sexual behavior. The fact that the First Amendment does not protect obscenity makes it easier for authorities to lock up people who make or consume child pornography. Regardless of what Americans think the term *obscenity* may mean where adult sexuality is concerned, few argue that child pornography should be protected speech. As in other scenarios, the drawbacks of extending First Amendment rights to child pornography strongly outweigh the benefits of doing so.

Nongovernment Consequences

There is a final situation in which free-speech protections do not typically apply, and that situation involves speech in the private sector. The First Amendment clearly states that Congress cannot make laws punishing those who speak freely. It does not, however, regulate what businesses, ordinary people, or other nongovernmental groups may do when faced with speech they do not like. Since these entities do not have the power to arrest or imprison speakers, the Constitution is silent about how they may react to the speech of others. Americans often believe that a person's free speech is being infringed when a private party, such as a corporation or a neighbor, responds punitively to that person's words. But that is not the case.

Indeed, corporations and other private entities frequently limit the speech of their employees or members in ways that the government cannot. A common example involves homeowners' associations (HOAs), private organizations run by groups of people who own property in a particular neighborhood or along a given street. To maintain order and uniformity, most HOAs require members to follow certain rules. In some cases these rules include bans on individual homeowners displaying political signs on their property. A city or state government would not be allowed to establish such a ban, and courts in some locations have limited the rights of HOAs to do so. But in most parts of the United States, there is broad agreement that HOAs, because they are private organizations, may restrict this kind of speech.

Some of the most famous cases of this type involve workers who have been fired because their employers disliked something the employee said. In 2015 and 2016, for example, sports broadcaster and retired baseball pitcher Curt Schilling used social media to circulate politically inflammatory images and statements. "He posted repulsive things to Facebook nearly every day," wrote one commentator, "continually dehumanizing others."[14] One of Schilling's tweets and memes suggested that presidential candidate Hillary Clinton be "buried under a jail somewhere,"[15] and another seemed to advocate that journalists be lynched. Complaints from sports fans and others who viewed Schilling's posts did nothing to change his ways; on the contrary, Schilling seemed to delight in being perceived as offensive.

Private Consequences

But Schilling's employer, sports network ESPN, eventually tired of Schilling's online activities. Concerned that Schilling was driving viewers away and recognizing that he did not reflect the values of the network, ESPN suspended him in late 2015. The suspension had little effect, though, since after reinstatement Schilling continued to post as before. In early 2016 Schilling put up a Facebook post that many readers considered especially offensive to transgender people. His employer lost no time addressing the situation. "ESPN is an inclusive company," the network explained in a statement. "Curt Schilling has been advised that his conduct was unacceptable and his employment with ESPN has been terminated."[16]

Many people were surprised, even angered, by ESPN's decision to fire Schilling. Some argued that Schilling's right to free speech was being infringed. According to the law, however, ESPN had every right to terminate Schilling. The government, after all, did not penalize Schilling for his speech in any way. He was not arrested, fined, or imprisoned for his tweets and Facebook posts. His employer, though, was not a government but a private business, and it could legally fire Schilling for almost any reason—including what Schilling said in forums that had little or nothing to do with his job duties. As a Pennsylvania newspaper editorial pointed out, "While the First Amendment guarantees freedom of speech . . . it does not guarantee freedom from consequences."[17]

People who are fired, suspended, or otherwise penalized for their words have no legal recourse if the punishment is carried out by a private actor such as a corporation. The Constitution, as noted, protects speech only from government reprisal. Still, many observers worry that free speech suffers when companies punish workers for comments unrelated to the workplace. They fear that some people may choose not to engage in any controversial speech to avoid the possibility of being fired. Such self-censorship, they point out, ultimately harms the free exchange of ideas. In this way the penalizing of certain types of speech by corporations can dampen free expression almost as much as the policing of speech by government. Writer Fredrik deBoer argues that "private employers can constitute a grave threat to our free speech rights."[18] Still, the law is clear: In general, workers who are fired for their ideas or manner of self-expression have no recourse on grounds of free speech.

> **"While the First Amendment guarantees freedom of speech . . . it does not guarantee freedom from consequences."[17]**
>
> — *York (PA) Dispatch* editorial

Despite what the Constitution suggests, speech is not always protected in modern America. Speech is rarely protected from consequences by private individuals or organizations, for example—only from government censorship. Even then, government does have the right to ban a few types of speech—notably those that maliciously harm other people's reputations, bring physical injury to others, or advocate immediate illegal action. The severity of these situations indicates that the harm caused by free speech must be great indeed for it to be suppressed. Unless there are serious consequences resulting from allowing people to speak freely, the expectation in the United States is that free speech is always permitted.

CHAPTER 2

Free Speech on Campus

The United States has hundreds of institutions of higher learning: famous colleges and universities known across the world, small community colleges serving the people of a single county, and everything in between. All of these colleges prepare students for advanced study or jobs that require specialized knowledge. But in the American mind, colleges often are given an importance that goes well beyond the importance of a high school or a middle school. The American college has often been referred to as a "marketplace of ideas"[19]—a place, removed from the rest of society, in which students, professors, and outside speakers can discuss ideas and beliefs in an atmosphere of openness, curiosity, and tolerance.

The likening of a college to a marketplace makes sense. Students participating in a free exchange of ideas, whether in or out of class, do in a sense take on the marketplace roles of seller and buyer. Those who have ideas to share are the sellers; those who adopt the ideas of others are the buyers. It is up to the sellers to convince the buyers that their ideas are worth hearing—and worth accepting. During this process, students come face-to-face with new perspectives and must find ways of incorporating what they learn into their view of the world. It can be a difficult and sometimes frustrating progression, but ideally students will hear diverse viewpoints, learn from one another, and allow new ways of thinking to influence their lives.

That, at any rate, is the ideal. But in some important ways, the colleges of today bear little resemblance to a true marketplace of ideas. Instead of listening with an open mind to the perspectives of others, quite a few college students—and occasional professors as well—seem determined to suppress speech they do not like. At many schools, outside speakers with unpopular opinions have been disinvited to give lectures; at others, those attempting to talk have been drowned out by shouts from the audience. Many colleges are also paying much closer attention to what students say in and out of class. They are increasingly likely to discipline students who use speech that might be considered offensive to others—regardless, in some cases, of what the First Amendment has to say.

The limiting of free speech on campuses is a concern for the vitality of colleges—and a potential issue for the continued success of America as well. "If the U.S. is to be a society that embraces the flourishing of ideas," writes commentator Charles Snow, "there may not be a more crucial place for free speech to thrive than the university." Yet if college students—the next generation of leaders—cannot come to value free speech, Snow points out, then the concept of freedom of speech itself may be in danger. "Students that learn simply to silence ideas they do not like," Snow continues, "will do the same when they leave the campus and enter the real world. . . . If those exiting college do not value the First Amendment, where will that leave our society?"[20]

> "If those exiting college do not value the First Amendment, where will that leave our society?"[20]
>
> —Writer Charles Snow

Public and Private Colleges

There are two types of colleges in America: public and private. Public colleges are heavily subsidized by state, city, or county governments and run by trustees who are directly answerable to government leaders. Like public elementary, middle, and high schools, public colleges are in effect an arm of the government. Well-known public colleges in the United States

College students protest President Donald Trump's policies on DACA at the University of California at Berkeley. Once considered places open to new ideas and discourse, some American colleges have begun to suppress unpopular views.

include the University of California–Los Angeles, North Carolina State University, and the University of Wisconsin. The list also includes many community colleges, which grant two-year degrees and often offer vocational classes, programs for children, and English courses for immigrants. These schools can be found in many counties across the country; Texas alone has more than sixty community colleges.

Private colleges, in contrast, receive little if any money from government sources. To stay in business, they rely on tuition and fees from students and on individual and corporate donors. Private colleges have a status similar to independent or religious schools in K–12 education; legally, they are not an arm of the government. Like public colleges, private colleges in the United States can be quite large or very small; some have no more than a few hundred students, while others have thousands. Well-known private colleges in the United States include Villanova University in Pennsylvania, Brigham Young University in Utah, and Oberlin College in Ohio.

Because of their different relationships to government, public and private colleges are treated differently where freedom of speech is concerned. Public schools, as a part of government, are subject to the First Amendment, so they may not restrict speech, except within the context of what the law exempts from the First Amendment. The different status of private colleges, however, allows them to restrict campus speech in ways that public schools cannot. The issues relating to colleges and free speech are much more pronounced with regard to public universities.

Still, private colleges enroll several million students at any given time, so the actions of private colleges have an enormous impact as well. While free-speech advocates are mostly concerned with limitations placed on speech at public colleges, they pay attention to free-speech issues at private colleges as well. As they see it, any unreasonable restriction on speech is a poor idea, and even if such a restriction is not specifically against the law, it should be addressed. Thus, the questions surrounding free speech on campus are not limited to public colleges alone.

Speech Zones

In the 1960s college students increasingly became politicized. Two issues in particular stood out: the civil rights movement, which the students generally supported, and the Vietnam War, which they strongly opposed. By the late 1960s students were holding frequent protest rallies at colleges across the nation, hoping to draw attention to their causes. In some places, they blocked sidewalks, streets, or entrances to classrooms while chanting and holding signs. College administrators generally disapproved of the protests to begin with, and they grew concerned when the protests began to disrupt ordinary campus life. Something, they decided, needed to be done.

The administrators' eventual response, in many cases, was to establish so-called free-speech zones. Within those zones, students could protest all they wanted, but protests would not be allowed elsewhere on campus. The idea was to keep students who were engaged in protest from interfering with day-to-day campus activities while still allowing them to express their opinions. College officials in general recognized that they could not censor students' words, but the law allowed them to limit when and where students could engage in controversial speech. Thus, the administrators who set up free-speech zones believed that they were not in violation of the First Amendment.

In many cases, though, they were wrong. Recently, students have challenged the constitutionality of free-speech zones at many colleges. Free-speech zones, they argue, imply that freedom of speech does not truly exist on the rest of campus. Thus, the students say, the zones are in violation of the First Amendment. Often, courts have agreed. In 2012, for instance, a federal court ruled that the free-speech zone at the University of Cincinnati—which took up 0.01 percent of the campus—was "so small that it would limit free expression."[21] In a similar case from 2004, Texas Tech University had set up a "free-speech gazebo," about 20 feet (6 m) wide, as the only place on campus where students could engage in protest. A judge overruled the college, stating that all public areas of the campus had to be opened to speech of all kinds. "The university's policies were among the biggest violations of the free speech rights of students that I have ever seen,"[22] said one lawyer.

Today, thanks in part to these lawsuits, free-speech zones at American colleges are much less common than they once were. In 2013 one college in six had designated free-speech zones; by 2016 the number had fallen to one in ten. Like judges, state

Students protest in a "free-speech zone" at Grand Valley State University in Michigan. To minimize disruption caused by protesting, many colleges have designated areas on campus as free-speech zones, where students are free to protest.

legislatures are taking a dim view of the practice. As of late 2017 at least seven states had passed laws banning such zones. Free-speech advocates applaud the dismantling of free-speech zones but believe that the pace of change is not enough. The number of colleges with speech zones has dropped, notes the Foundation for Individual Rights in Education (FIRE), a free-speech advocacy group. But, according to FIRE, the number of existing speech zones "is still unacceptably high considering [that] such policies are inconsistent with the First Amendment."[23]

Speech Codes and Hate Speech

Free-speech zones may be disappearing, but other infringements of free speech on college campuses have taken their place. In the

Campus Speech Codes Violate Free Speech Rights

The American Association of University Professors has taken a strong stance in favor of protecting all kinds of speech, even offensive speech, on college campuses. This is an excerpt from a position paper on the issue.

> Freedom of thought and expression is essential to any institution of higher learning. Universities and colleges exist not only to transmit knowledge. Equally, they interpret, explore, and expand that knowledge by testing the old and proposing the new. This mission guides learning outside the classroom quite as much as in class, and often inspires vigorous debate on those social, economic, and political issues that arouse the strongest passions. In the process, views will be expressed that may seem to many wrong, distasteful, or offensive. Such is the nature of freedom to sift and winnow ideas.
>
> On a campus that is free and open, no idea can be banned or forbidden. No viewpoint or message may be deemed so hateful or disturbing that it may not be expressed.

AAUP, "On Freedom of Expression and Campus Speech Codes." www.aaup.org/report/freedom-expression-and-campus-speech-codes.

late 1980s, for example, many American colleges experienced a wave of hate speech—offensive comments directed at people because of their race, gender, national origin, or religion. Most of the hate speech was aimed at women, racial minorities, or people from low socioeconomic levels, and much of it came from wealthier white males. The victims of this speech complained to college administrators, whose response, in many cases, was to institute a speech code—a set of guidelines that banned certain kinds of speech from campus. The University of Michigan, for example, barred students from using speech that "demeans or stigmatizes"[24] people because of their gender or race.

Speech codes quickly became common among American universities. Just seventy-five colleges had speech codes in 1990; a year later the figure was over three hundred, and the number rose rapidly as the decade wore on. On one level, the codes did exactly what administrators intended. The codes helped remind students to treat each other with respect, and establishing clear rules

Campus Speech Codes Do Not Violate Free Speech Rights

An editorial that appeared in the student newspaper of Wellesley College in Massachusetts argues that rules against hate speech do not infringe on free speech.

> Many members of our community . . . have criticized [Wellesley] for becoming an environment where free speech is not allowed or is a violated right. Many outside sources have painted us as a bunch of hot house flowers who cannot exist in the real world. However, we fundamentally disagree with that characterization, and we disagree with the idea that free speech is infringed upon at Wellesley. Rather, our Wellesley community will not stand for hate speech, and will call it out when possible. . . .
>
> Shutting down rhetoric that undermines the existence and rights of others is not a violation of free speech; it is hate speech. The founding fathers put free speech in the Constitution as a way to protect the disenfranchised and to protect individual citizens from the power of the government. The spirit of free speech is to protect the suppressed, not to protect a free-for-all where anything is acceptable, no matter how hateful and damaging.

"Free Speech Is Not Violated at Wellesley," *Wellesley News*, April 12, 2017. http://thewellesleynews.com.

allowed administrators to punish those who did not. Supporters of speech codes also pointed out that the codes helped redress some of the imbalances of power in society. "Speech has great power," writes a student at Harvard University. "It can—and often does—serve as a tool to marginalize and oppress people. Laws that restrict hate speech simply seek to prevent violence against marginalized, oppressed groups in order to prevent them from becoming further marginalized and oppressed."[25] If hateful speech is considered a form of violence, and if speech codes diminish hateful speech, then speech codes are effective.

> "Laws that restrict hate speech simply seek to prevent violence against marginalized, oppressed groups in order to prevent them from becoming further marginalized and oppressed."[25]
>
> —Student journalist at Harvard University

On another level, though, speech codes are problematic. One issue is that speech codes are often vaguely written. Dartmouth College in New Hampshire, for example, at one point banned students from posting words online that were "harmful, offensive [or] abusive."[26] These descriptors are exceptionally imprecise: Speech that one person views as harmful may seem perfectly acceptable to someone else. Nor is it clear that speech codes have consistently protected the rights of minorities or other marginalized groups. "During the years Michigan's speech code was on the books," notes free-speech advocate Erwin Chemerinsky, "more than 20 black students were charged with racist speech by white students. There wasn't a single instance of a white student being punished for racist speech."[27]

The bigger issue, however, is legal: Nearly all speech codes at public universities are in violation of the First Amendment. The Constitution protects most forms of speech, and speech that is merely offensive or even abusive is among them. In contrast, the Constitution says nothing about bruised feelings, racist language, or marginalization. When free speech collides with people's desire to feel safe within a college community, the legal question is settled. There is a constitutional guarantee of a right to freedom of speech, but there is no equivalent right for people to feel safe. Unless public college speech codes only ban language that is not protected by the Constitution—and very few do—they are not acceptable from a legal perspective.

In recent years, colleges have begun to move away from speech codes. Free-speech organizations such as FIRE have pointed out the contradictions between speech codes and free-speech rights, and colleges are listening. Between 2008 and 2018, the number of colleges with speech codes has dropped every year. Some schools, indeed, have strongly affirmed a commitment to free speech, even at the cost of permitting speech that may be offensive. "Members of our community are encouraged to speak, write, listen, challenge, and learn, without fear of censorship,"[28] wrote University of Chicago dean John Ellison in 2016. Still, about a third of the universities surveyed by FIRE in early 2018 had a speech code still in place. The threat presented to freedom of speech by university speech codes is not over.

Campus Speakers

Another issue regarding free speech on college campuses has to do with outside speakers. College academic departments and student organizations sometimes invite people from outside the school to give a lecture open to faculty and students. These speakers may be scholars at other institutions, but they also can be journalists, business leaders, politicians, and others who are prominent in their fields. Most speakers are not especially well known, and their time on campus attracts relatively little attention. In recent years, however, some speakers have generated a great deal of controversy—to the point that members of the community have demanded that the invitation be rescinded. This, of course, brings up important questions about the limits of free speech.

One of the most famous of these controversies took place at the University of California–Berkeley in 2017. Students and faculty at most American campuses are more likely to be liberal than conservative, and left-wing views are especially common at Berkeley. That spring, however, a group of conservative students invited right-wing commentators Ann Coulter and Milo Yiannopoulos to give lectures at the Berkeley campus. Both Coulter and Yiannopoulos are known for their strident rhetoric; one of Coulter's books bears the provocative title *Demonic: How the Liberal Mob Is Endangering America*, and Yiannopoulos's opinions include the notion that transgender people are mentally ill. The news that speakers such as Coulter and Yiannopoulos were going to speak dismayed many progressives on campus and in the community, and some immediately set out to stop the speeches from taking place.

They succeeded. When Yiannopoulos arrived, he was met by hundreds of protesters. The great majority attacked Yiannopoulos with speech, speaking out peacefully against the speaker's presence on the campus, but other protesters responded to the lecture with violence. They broke windows and set fires on campus and in the surrounding community, eventually causing the university to cancel the speech because of safety concerns. Coulter's speech, scheduled for a few weeks afterward, was likewise canceled when the university decided it could not keep people safe; school officials had received credible messages threatening violence if Coulter were allowed to speak on campus. "Ann Coulter is welcome on this campus," said a university spokesperson, "but [only] at a time when we can provide a venue that law enforcement professionals believe to be protectable."[29]

The decision to disinvite the conservative speakers outraged many on the right. They feared that the concern about violence was merely an excuse designed to cover the fact that the college had a strong bias against conservativism. More generally, they

In 2017, the University of California at Berkeley canceled a lecture on campus scheduled to be given by conservative pundit Ann Coulter (pictured). University officials had received credible threats of violence if Coulter was allowed to speak on campus.

worried that campus administrators were unfairly restricting the free speech of the planned visitors. "Our society can't have civil discourse, can't have debate," said conservative student Mike Wright, "if we choose to silence ourselves because of the threat of fringe groups."[30] Conservative student groups pressed to reschedule the speakers. They eventually got permission to invite several conservative speakers to campus for an event in the fall. But once again there were threats of violence, and most of the speeches were canceled.

Shouting Speakers Down

Other schools have experienced similar controversies, mostly but not exclusively involving right-wing speakers. In some cases speakers were disinvited, much as happened at Berkeley. Trinity College in Connecticut invited rapper Action Bronson to speak, for example, and then rescinded the invitation when student groups complained that his lyrics were misogynistic (meaning they demonstrate hatred toward women). Williams College in Massachusetts revoked a speaking engagement extended to social critic Suzanne Venker, who calls herself an antifeminist, and similarly disinvited John Derbyshire, a journalist who once counseled white people, including his children, to "stay out of heavily black neighborhoods."[31] And California State University, Los Angeles, disinvited conservative writer Ben Shapiro when members of the college community argued that his views on Black Lives Matter and other topics were unacceptable.

In other cases speakers did present their lectures, but students and others attempted to stifle their message by interrupting them repeatedly while they spoke. At the University of Florida, for example, white nationalist Richard Spencer gave a controversial speech in late 2017. Many students turned out to jeer him, booing him loudly and chanting "Go home Spencer"[32] as he gave his speech. Claire Gastañaga, a speaker from the ACLU, an organization noted for its support of free speech even for those whose views are unpopular, was similarly shouted down as she gave a lecture at the College of William & Mary in Virginia in late 2017. Perhaps ironically, Gastañaga was arguing in favor of free speech, but some students were irate that she had been invited. "ACLU, you protect Hitler, too," students shouted, along with other comments such as "the oppressed are not impressed."[33] After half an hour the event was canceled because the speaker could not make herself heard over the noise.

"Silencing certain voices in order to advance the cause of others is not acceptable in our community."[34]

—Taylor Reveley, president of the College of William & Mary

For free-speech advocates, incidents like these are troubling—even if they occur at private colleges such as Trinity and Williams, but especially if they take place at public universities. Indeed, many college administrators recognize that suppressing speakers through heckling, threats of violence, or canceling invitations sets a bad precedent. "Silencing certain voices in order to advance the cause of others is not acceptable in our community," writes William & Mary president Taylor Reveley. "This stifles debate and prevents those who've come to hear a speaker . . . from engaging in debate where the strength of ideas, not the power of shouting, is the currency."[34] Likewise, University of Florida president W. Kent Fuchs, while stating that he despised Spencer's ideas, noted that the Constitution did not allow the university to keep him from speaking. Fuchs advised students not to try to prevent Spencer from delivering a speech, but rather to "shun Spencer and to speak against his message of hate and racism."[35]

> "Challenge those you disagree with. More speech, not less, is always the best retaliation against ignorance."[36]
>
> —Student journalist Lili Carneglia

Fuchs's point is that the solution to the problem of speech that is unpopular, offensive, or even hateful is not to disinvite those with different points of view. Nor is it to shout them down or to fight back against them physically. Rather, it is to attack their message with more speech—with words that are more accurate, more compassionate, and more effective. The goal is to point out where—and why—the offending speech is wrong, and to offer a better replacement. As University of Alabama student journalist Lili Carneglia puts it, "Challenge those you disagree with. More speech, not less, is always the best retaliation against ignorance."[36]

CHAPTER 3

Artistic Expression

In many societies throughout human history, art produced for public consumption—paintings, architecture, poetry, and so on—has been sharply regulated. Works of art that did not appeal to society's leaders, or works that threatened their authority in some way, were censored: banned, burned, or hacked to pieces. Sometimes the censorship was aimed only at specific works or at certain artists. In 8 CE, for instance, government officials in Rome decided that a book called *The Art of Love*, written by a poet named Ovid, was morally offensive. Government leaders destroyed as many copies of the book as they could find and, for good measure, exiled Ovid to Greece. Another example comes from 1597, when William Shakespeare published his play *Richard III*. Shakespeare's original script included a scene in which a king was forcibly removed from power. The queen of England at the time, Elizabeth I, believed that the scene represented an unacceptable attack on the monarchy. She ordered that it be excised from all copies of the script, and she barred performance of the scene anywhere within the country.

In other cases directives against works of art have been much broader. A Chinese emperor known as Shihuangdi, for example, supposedly ordered the burning of nearly every book in his kingdom in 213 BCE. In 1933 members of the newly powerful Nazi Party in Germany burned thousands of books written by Communists, Jews, and other authors—including a number of German writers—whose worldviews were contrary to the Nazis' own. And for many years the

United Kingdom had a law giving enormous power to a government functionary, the lord chamberlain, in determining what British theater audiences could and could not see. Anyone who wished to perform a play in the country had to submit a copy of the script to the lord chamberlain, who could choose to censor the work or prevent it from being shown. Though this authority was rarely exercised after 1900 or so, the law remained on the books until 1968.

Pictured is a scene from William Shakespeare's play *Richard III*. The queen of England ordered that a scene from the play, which she believed was an attack on the monarchy, be permanently removed.

The United States

The United States, too, has had many instances in which governments have tried to forbid the publication, display, or performance of artworks deemed unacceptable in some way. Sculptures, books, rap songs, photographs, and many other forms of art have been challenged and sometimes banned by officials at all levels of government. In this aspect the United States is not that dissimilar to ancient Rome, Elizabethan England, or imperial China, where censorship of art was common and indeed expected. But there is one significant difference between these societies and the modern United States, and that is the American commitment in law and in custom to free speech. Unlike Elizabeth I or Adolf Hitler, American leaders have a legal duty to balance the rights of artists to express themselves freely against the potential harm they could cause the government and the people who support it.

Governments in the United States very rarely have the power—or indeed the desire—to completely ban an artwork or artistic medium. In the United States controversies about artistic expression most often revolve around the question of who should be able to access a work, not the question of whether the work should exist at all. Though there are exceptions, those who would like to limit artistic expression generally do not call for the arrest of the people who create or perform certain works or suggest that publishing companies or music distributors be shut down for producing potentially offensive material. Instead, they focus on getting books removed from public libraries, closing art exhibitions, and pressuring retailers not to sell certain video games. For the most part, these are limited and sometimes isolated actions that do not seriously affect an artist's ability to make money or become better known.

But even if the impact does not seem great, in the long run any restrictions on a book, a painting, or a song may have the effect of limiting free artistic expression. When a radio station decides not to play a song that some consider offensive, for example, the composer and performer lose out on royalties. They also suffer in comparison to less controversial artists because casual listeners to the station will not hear the full range of their work. In some cases artists may lose grant money if they engage in unpopular speech. Alternatively, they may not be given serious consideration for future grants. Moreover, challenges to creative works may make publishers, music producers, and museums less willing to invest in art that might prove controversial. Even if government does not take steps to ban a given artwork outright, attacks of any kind on artistic expression may ultimately limit speech.

Challenges to Art

The list of artistic works challenged by governments and ordinary Americans in recent years is long. Many of these are books, especially books intended for curricular use. In New York State, classroom use of the children's book *Al Capone Does My Shirts* was challenged because, complainants argued, the book promoted negative stereotypes regarding Italian Americans. (School officials did not agree and kept the book in the curriculum.) An Idaho school district considered removing John Steinbeck's classic novel *Of Mice and Men* from the curriculum when parents objected to the book's language and negative outlook, though again the school board ultimately did not remove the book. J.D. Salinger's *Catcher in the Rye*, Harper Lee's *To Kill a Mockingbird*, and Alice Walker's *The Color Purple* are also classic novels that have been frequently challenged.

While challenges to books often fail, they can also be successful. Mark Haddon's best-selling novel *The Curious Incident of the Dog in the Night-Time*, for example, has been challenged because of scenes in which characters use swear words and because of what some have called an atheistic worldview. "To have that language [that is, swearing] and to take the name of Christ in vain—I don't go for that," said a Florida woman who was upset that her daughter, a high school student, was required to read the

The list of artistic works challenged by governments and ordinary Americans in recent years is long. Author J.D. Salinger's classic novel *Catcher in the Rye* has been frequently challenged.

novel. "As a Christian, and as a female, I was offended."[37] In 2015 the novel was removed from at least two reading lists at American high schools as a result of concerns like these.

Banning and censorship are not limited to books. In 2017, for instance, a school in San Jose, California, displayed a series of eleven paintings by an artist who lived nearby. The paintings were in celebration of Black History Month and focused on racial injustice. Several parents complained about the display, however, because they believed it took a political stance, and they thought that political messages were inappropriate in a school setting. The district superintendent agreed and removed the paintings. That same year, a theater group in Burnsville, Minnesota, asked city officials for permission to present a play in a city-owned performing arts center. The title of the play included a word that many people considered to be racist, and city officials refused to allow the play to be presented. "I feel it's a derogatory term and it's extremely offensive,"[38] said Brian Luther, director of the center.

Video games have also been the subject of censorship. That is especially true of material with substantial violence or sexual content. Some especially violent video games have come under attack from people who believe they should not be available to the public. In a famous example from 2009, Christine Quinn, then the Speaker of the New York City Council, denounced a video game in which the player sets out to rape women. The game, Quinn said, was "absolutely horrifying."[39] In response, Amazon and other major retail outlets in the United States agreed to stop selling the game. The ban was not complete: The game was still available on the Internet, and owning or buying a copy of the game was never made illegal. Still, those who were disgusted by the game considered the outcome a victory.

Conservative and Liberal Objections

The reasons why people advocate restrictions on certain works of art are varied, but in general the attacks on artistic expression come from two very different perspectives. One group consists largely of conservative Christians with a strict moral code based on their understanding of the Bible. To them, much of today's art, from the vulgar language used in rap music to the prevalence of pornographic images on the Internet, damages the moral fabric of society. People in this group see modern America as a place where artists aim mainly to shock rather than to create works of beauty. They worry that millions of Americans now see profanity and explicit references to sex not as something to be avoided but rather as normal parts of everyday life.

Conservative activists concerned about inappropriateness in art often focus their objections on the effect of art on young people, especially teenagers. In one recent example, New York parents Patti and Aldo DeVivo raised strong objections to the use of a novel called *The Perks of Being a Wallflower* as assigned

School Boards May Not Remove Books from Libraries

In the 1982 case *Board of Education v. Pico*, the US Supreme Court ruled that a school board could not remove books from the school library because board members found the books offensive. This is an excerpt from the majority opinion written by Justice William Brennan.

> Local school boards have broad discretion in the management of school affairs, but such discretion must be exercised in a manner that comports with the transcendent imperatives of the First Amendment. . . .
>
> Petitioners [that is, school board members] possess significant discretion to determine the content of their school libraries, but that discretion may not be exercised in a narrowly partisan or political manner. . . . Local school boards may not remove books from school libraries simply because they dislike the ideas contained in those books and seek by their removal to "prescribe what shall be orthodox in politics, nationalism, religion, or other matters of opinion."

Quoted in *New York Times*, "Excerpts from Justices' Opinions on Island Trees, L.I., School Library Suit," June 26, 1982. www.nytimes.com.

reading in their daughter's high school English class. The DeVivos were appalled by many aspects of the novel, notably frequent use of profanity, descriptions of sexual behavior, and references to drug use, abortion, and homosexuality. Concerned that reading the book might warp young people's ideas of right and wrong and lead students to make poor choices, the DeVivos tried unsuccessfully to get the novel removed from the curriculum. The couple's opposition to the book was deep rooted. When asked whether *The Perks of Being a Wallflower* should be relegated to the school library rather than being used as a classroom text, Pat-

School Boards May Remove Books from Libraries

The Supreme Court was sharply divided in the *Pico* case. Chief Justice Warren Burger argued that the school board did have the right to remove books from the school library. An excerpt from his dissenting opinion follows.

> [N]o restraints of any kind are placed on the students. They are free to read the books in question, which are available at public libraries and bookstores; they are free to discuss them in the classroom or elsewhere. . . .
>
> If, as we have held, schools may legitimately be used as vehicles for inculcating fundamental values necessary to the maintenance of a democratic political system, school authorities must have broad discretion to fulfill that obligation. . . . How are "fundamental values" to be inculcated except by having school boards make content-based decisions about the appropriateness of retaining materials in the school library and curriculum.

Quoted in *New York Times*, "Excerpts from Justices' Opinions on Island Trees, L.I., School Library Suit," June 26, 1982. www.nytimes.com/1982/06/26/us/excerpts-from-justices-opinions-on-island-trees-li-school-library-suit.html?pagewanted=all.

ti DeVivo's response was blunt. "I believe it doesn't belong anywhere," she said. "It belongs in the garbage can."[40]

Not everyone who seeks to censor art shares the political and religious views of the DeVivos. Others lean to the left politically; they object to artistic works not because of traditional ideas of morality but rather for different reasons. One of these focuses on the question of authenticity, or the connection between artist and subject matter. A 2017 exhibition at the

"I believe it doesn't belong anywhere. It belongs in the garbage can."[40]

—Parent Patty DeVivo about a novel her daughter was assigned to read

Whitney Museum of American Art in New York City, for instance, featured a painting called *Open Casket*. Created by American artist Dana Schutz, the work depicted the funeral of African American teenager Emmett Till, who was savagely beaten and lynched by white racists in Mississippi in 1955. But because Schutz was white, not African American, some artists argued that she had no right to retell Till's story in her art. They urged the museum to close the exhibition or remove Schutz's painting; a few demanded that the work be destroyed. "It's not acceptable for a white person to transmute Black suffering into profit and fun,"[41] says an artist named Hannah Black.

Progressives who advocate censoring works of art they deem offensive also may object to artworks that feed into ethnic, gender, or racial stereotypes or could be hurtful to vulnerable or marginalized people. In 2017, for example, a woman named Mia Merrill started an online petition urging the Metropolitan Museum of Art in New York City to remove a painting called *Therese Dreaming*. The painting depicted a young girl in an erotic pose. The subject matter distressed Merrill, who calls herself a progressive feminist. At the time, sexual harassment cases were dominating the news, with allegations of wrongdoing being leveled against celebrities ranging from movie producer Harvey Weinstein to radio personality Garrison Keillor. Against this backdrop, Merrill believed that it was wrong to continue displaying the work. "This painting is undeniably romanticizing the sexualization of a child," her petition reads. "Given the current climate around sexual assault . . . the Met is romanticizing voyeurism and the objectification of children."[42]

There is one point on which conservatives and liberals worried about artistic expression often agree, and that is the connection between violence in the media and real-life violence. Many people across the political spectrum are deeply concerned about the effects on children of watching violent movies and playing gory video games. They cite studies that suggest a correlation between screen violence and aggression, and they note that several high-profile mass murderers have identified video games as an influence for their actions. In particular, they worry that viewing extensive screen violence distorts young people's understanding of reality. "I honestly believed that if you shoot somebody, that they would get back up," says Evan Ramsey, who shot four people at his Alaska high

> "I honestly believed that if you shoot somebody, that they would get back up."[43]
>
> —School shooter Evan Ramsey

school in 1997. Ramsey notes that in violent video games, it often takes multiple shots before the target is dead. "I didn't realize that [when] you shoot somebody [in real life], they die."[43]

Free-Speech Advocacy

Whether coming from a liberal perspective or a more conservative one, many Americans fundamentally believe that protecting artistic expression—in at least some cases—is less important than protecting members of the public from art that they might find offensive. Other Americans, however, vociferously disagree with this perspective. Free-speech supporters use several different arguments to make their case. Advocates of free artistic expression argue, for example, that the nation is best served when art of all kinds is accepted or at least tolerated. "In order to have a truly free society, we must have freedom of artistic expression—an unbridled creativity that is devoid of all forms of censorship," writes artist Julie Trébault. "The world needs art to help us not only see beyond difference, but also to understand it."[44]

> "In order to have a truly free society, we must have freedom of artistic expression—an unbridled creativity that is devoid of all forms of censorship."[44]
>
> —Artist Julie Trébault

Supporters of free speech also point out that some of the world's most revered artworks were harshly criticized when they first appeared. For example, many sixteenth-century viewers complained about Michelangelo's 1565 painting *The Last Judgment*

Free speech supporters point out that some of the world's most cherished artworks were challenged when they first appeared. Michelangelo's 1565 painting *The Last Judgement* (pictured) was initially criticized because some figures were naked.

because some of the figures were naked. "Not even in the brothel are there such scenes as yours,"[45] one contemporary poet told the artist. Today the painting is considered a masterpiece. *Leaves of Grass*, a collection of poems by American writer Walt Whitman, was scheduled to be published in Boston in 1881. The local district attorney, however, threatened to prosecute the publisher because of vulgar language in several of the poems. The volume was published in Philadelphia the following year and became a classic. Free-speech advocates note that *The Last Judgment* and *Leaves of Grass* might have been lost forever if the would-be censors had had their way.

Free-speech advocates also argue that censorship invariably has a negative effect on the artistic world. As complaints and challenges against works of art mount, artists, museums, and publishers become less likely to push the boundaries. When a book such as *The Perks of Being a Wallflower* is challenged, publishing companies may be reluctant to put out a similarly controversial novel. When the political content of an artist's work makes it impossible for him or her to get a grant, other artists may decide to eliminate political content in their own creations. In this way, censorship of any kind has "a chilling effect on artists and art organizations,"[46] as authors Richard L. Lewis and Susan Ingalls Lewis put it. The world, they argue, would be a poorer place if artists began censoring themselves.

Media and Behavior

Another pro-free-speech argument touches on the concerns expressed by many Americans that violent or indecent material may corrupt young minds. Defenders of artistic expression argue that it is very difficult to show a strong connection between a person's consumption of art—be it books, music, paintings, or video games—and that person's actions. That is particularly true for images involving nudity or even explicit sex. Pornography, free-speech advocates maintain, may be in poor taste, but it does not cause viewers to commit sexual assault. "No causal link between exposure to sexually explicit material and anti-social or violent behavior has ever been scientifically established,"[47] points out the ACLU.

The evidence is less clear where violent movies and games are concerned. Free-speech advocates acknowledge that aggressive behavior has sometimes been linked to violent movies and video games, but they note that this does not imply that violent media leads to aggression. It is possible, they point out, that the connection works in the opposite direction: The link may indicate only that violent people like to play violent video games and watch violent movies. In any case, many studies conclude that there is no evidence suggesting that violence in the media influences behavior in any way. "We've tried hard for decades to find links between media and societal violence," says researcher Christopher Ferguson. "If they were a major cause of problems in society we'd know by now. But the evidence just isn't there."[48]

From the perspective of those who support artistic expression, moreover, creative works such as books, movies, and video games simply do not have the power to fundamentally change someone's outlook and personality. While it is true that teenagers often try out different identities, these identities are not necessarily influenced by what adolescents watch, read, and play. "Reading about a gay character does not make [readers] gay," points out Wisconsin librarian Kristin Pekoll; "reading about drinking and driving does not make them want to drink and drive."[49] Only a tiny fraction of people who play violent video games ever murder anyone, free-speech advocates note. Nor is there much evidence that the gaming is the most significant contributor to violent actions. Most studies suggest that bullying, mental health issues, and other factors are much more significant.

Constitutional Guarantees

For most free-speech advocates, however, the main justification for protecting artistic expression is the Constitution. The First Amendment says specifically that speech is protected from government interference. It says nothing about people being protected from images, stories, or video games they find offensive. Thus, to free-speech advocates, the constitutionally guaranteed right to free speech—even unpopular or offensive speech—must necessarily outweigh the desire to avoid such speech. As Supreme Court justice William Brennan put it, "If there is a bedrock principle underlying the First Amendment, it is that Government may not prohibit the expression of an idea simply because society finds the idea itself offensive or disagreeable."[50]

Indeed, courts have typically ruled in favor of free-speech advocates in cases revolving around artistic expression. One important precedent was set in 1982, when the US Supreme Court decided a case known as *Board of Education v. Pico*. A school board in New York voted to remove eleven books from the middle and high school libraries on the grounds that the books were "anti-American, anti-Christian, anti-Semitic, and just plain filthy." Several students, opposed to the decision, sued to have the books returned to the shelves. The court ruled that the guarantee of freedom of speech in the First Amendment overruled the wishes of school officials. As the majority opinion put it, "Local school boards may not remove books from school library shelves simply because they dislike the ideas contained in those books."[51]

Since 1982, then, it has been difficult for those who would like to ban books to win court cases, and indeed they rarely have. More generally, courts have followed the Constitution and sided with free-speech advocates wherever artistic expression is concerned. In a 1999 case, for instance, New York City mayor Rudy Giuliani was appalled by an exhibit at the Brooklyn Museum of Art, which received funding from the city as part of its budget. Giuliani was especially perturbed by a painting of the Virgin Mary in which the figure was partly hidden by elephant dung. Giuliani pushed the museum to cancel the exhibit. When museum officials refused, the mayor withheld $500,000 in funds for the museum. The museum sued, charging that Giuliani was engaging in illegal censorship under the First Amendment, and the courts agreed.

> "If there is a bedrock principle underlying the First Amendment, it is that Government may not prohibit the expression of an idea simply because society finds the idea itself offensive or disagreeable."[50]
>
> —Supreme Court justice William Brennan

This is not to say that cases like these are always decided in favor of free speech. But in the battle between free speech and censorship of art in the United States, the courts have usually ruled in accordance with the First Amendment. While some private citizens, elected politicians, and government bureaucrats have attempted to limit artistic freedom, in the long run they have not been successful. As the ACLU puts it, "The commitment to freedom of imagination and expression is deeply embedded in our national psyche."[52]

CHAPTER 4

Free Speech and the Internet

Few inventions of the past fifty years have been as influential as the Internet. Through Skype, e-mail, and social media, the Internet keeps people in touch across even long distances. The Internet is a treasure trove of information; thanks to search engines and online encyclopedias, it is possible to find data about almost any topic imaginable with just a few clicks of a mouse or taps on a screen. And the Internet has made all sorts of human endeavors easier: comparing the costs of plane tickets, determining where the latest blockbuster movie is playing, finding the quickest route between the park and the shopping mall.

The Internet, in its original inception, also seemed to offer other possibilities. Before the Internet, the media was dominated by television, radio, newspapers, and magazines. To many observers, these media outlets seemed staid and boring. Most were owned by large corporations concerned with their image, and they tended to be focused on not offending their audiences. Government, moreover, pressured these corporations to keep their content clean and inoffensive. As a result, vulgar or profane language was typically censored by most forms of media, along with images that might strike viewers as indecent. Unpopular points of view, similarly, were often not covered by newspapers or television stations.

In contrast, the Internet appeared to be something very different—a freewheeling place where people could write and post what they wanted without any government agency or powerful corporation attempting to stop it. And in its first years, that was the case. The Internet was often referred to as a modern version of the Wild West; in the words of one commentator, it was "a territory too new for rules to be drawn."[53] Websites went up with all manner of material that would never have been allowed in the pages of *Newsweek* or on a major broadcast network, though some did appear on cable television channels. These included offensive and violent language, explicit sex, depictions of intense violence, and opinions that were decidedly out of the mainstream. For some, the Internet was the only place where the promise of freedom of speech was still being kept.

But in recent years that has begun to change. Social media companies have grown from tiny start-ups to enormous corporations more receptive to the complaints of offended customers. Social media users have at the same time become more demanding about what they want to see online—and what they do not want to see. During 2016 and 2017 social media users began to complain vociferously about content distributed on sites such as Facebook and Twitter. One concern was the prevalence of fake news items appearing on these sites. Another was the amount of hate-filled speech. Several social media sites responded to the pressure by banning or restricting certain types of speech. But whether this is the best response is unclear, and some free-speech advocates have pushed back. One thing is clear: The battle is by no means over.

Fake News and Misinformation

In the run-up to the 2016 presidential election, social media sites became deluged with articles that appeared to be news items but were not. Rather, they were deliberate fakes, designed to look and read like a legitimate news story but with no basis in fact. Many of these fake news stories were intended to influence the election by disseminating stories that reflected badly on one of the candidates. One story, for example, claimed that Hillary Clinton and members of her staff had kidnapped children to use as prostitutes and were keeping them in the basement of a pizza restaurant in Washington, DC. "We're talking an international child enslavement and sex ring,"[54] someone using the name Carmen Katz tweeted shortly before the election. The story was a complete lie, but many social media users believed it—and they circulated it around the Internet as if it were true.

Lies have been told about public figures for years, and even legitimate newspapers are not above printing material their editors believe or even know to be wrong. But the modern phenomenon of fake news is different, in large part because the Internet has an enormous reach. In one survey of social media users from December 2016, almost half the respondents said they encountered fake news items at least once a day. And most people agree that fake news items create major issues for society. They may affect elections; it is possible that Clinton's loss to Donald Trump in 2016

Fake news has become a real issue for society. Some experts believe that Hillary Clinton's loss to Donald Trump in the 2016 presidential election was due in part to fake news items that hurt Clinton.

was due in part to fake news items that convinced wavering voters to choose her opponent. Fake news items also diminish trust in the media at large. If one article that looks like a legitimate news story turns out to be false, readers may conclude that many other articles are equally false—even when they turn out to be true.

The problem of fake news was made even more complex when law enforcement officials revealed that Russian operatives had used social media in other ways to influence and disrupt the 2016 election. "Fake personas were created on Facebook and elsewhere to amplify news accounts,"[55] Facebook admitted in a report. Russian workers, it turned out, had signed up for Facebook accounts. Some created individuals; others pretended to be organizations. The goal was to make other posters believe they were ordinary Americans concerned about the policies of the country. Thus, the names of the fake accounts sounded thoroughly American. One of the organizations, known as Heart of Texas, not only urged that Texas secede from the Union but posted a great deal of anti-immigrant rhetoric as well. At one point it had 225,000 followers.

These fake accounts also arranged to send false and misleading information to voters in key states. For example, a Russian account posing as an American organization identified Facebook users who were especially interested in veterans' issues. Then the account sent information to these people stating that Clinton did not support the military and describing how a Clinton presidency would be a disaster for the troops—and by extension, the country as a whole. Much of what they sent, however, was a deliberate misrepresentation of Clinton's actual position on military affairs. As with fake news, no one knows just how much influence these misinformation campaigns had on the election; but most observers would agree that any influence at all is too much.

Fake News and Free Speech

It took time for investigators to unravel the truth behind fake news and Russian interference in the election, especially where social

Facebook founder Mark Zuckerberg (pictured) at first dismissed the notion that social media had any role in spreading misinformation during the 2016 US presidential election. Facebook later changed its algorithms to make it easier to detect false stories.

media was concerned. Facebook's cofounder, Mark Zuckerberg, at first dismissed the notion that social media had any role in spreading misinformation. "I think the idea that fake news on Facebook—of which it's a small amount of content—influenced the election in any way is a pretty crazy idea,"[56] he said in November 2016. But Zuckerberg was wrong. And once the extent of the meddling was known, social media users and others began to clamor for social media sites to take steps to lessen the impact of misinformation and fake news.

To at least some degree, social media companies are doing just that. Twitter banned several thousand users after discovering that they were linked to a Russian group dedicated to spreading misinformation. Twitter also removed ads purchased on its site by certain Russian companies. Facebook, in turn, has changed its algorithms to make it easier to detect fake news, and it has hired fact-checkers to determine whether certain articles are factual.

Social Media Companies Threaten Free Speech

Natasha Tusikov, an expert on government regulation of the Internet, says that social media organizations such as Twitter and Facebook are complicit in the spread of fake news. Tusikov fears that encouraging these companies to regulate the speech of their members will reduce the speech rights of Americans.

> With so much at stake, it may be time for a fundamental rethink of how these indispensable 21st century companies are regulated and what they're allowed to do.

> At the very minimum, governments and citizens should reconsider whether the lack of oversight into how these companies shape our speech rights is really in the public interest.

> Social media platforms "are an enabler of democracy," says Margrethe Vestager, the European Union's Commissioner for Competition, but we're seeing that "they can also be used against our very basic beliefs in democracy."

> It's time to start taking that threat to democracy seriously.

Natasha Tusikov, "Regulate Social Media Platforms Before It's Too Late," The Conversation, November 6, 2017. theconversation.com.

Several social media companies have made it clear that users run the risk of being banned if they routinely pass on articles that have been identified as fake news.

These measures certainly can help reduce the spread of fake news online. At the same time, though, the actions of social media companies in this regard raise concerns about freedom of speech. No matter how good its algorithms, Facebook will of necessity make mistakes in identifying what is fake news and what

Social Media Companies Do Not Threaten Free Speech

Journalist Ankita Rao, who covers issues involving technology, points out in the following article excerpts that social media companies do not need to adhere to the First Amendment. Further, she also argues that these companies do a reasonable job of balancing the speech rights of their members with the desire of other members not to be offended.

> While public hate speech can't—and shouldn't, I think—be suppressed, social platforms like Twitter, Facebook, and Reddit are allowed to set their own restrictions to moderate the community they want to foster on their platforms. Using racial slurs or sexist language is protected in public life, but private companies can decide what kind of dialogue they will entertain.
>
> Twitter's new guidelines . . . demonstrate the company's latest reaction to constant reports of abuse and cyberbullying. The platform allows users to report hateful conversations, block racial slurs and opt out of whole conversations in an attempt to distance abusers from their victims. Think of it as a mechanism to control who steps into your home, versus the inevitability of encountering strangers on the street—which is important for those of us who have dealt with online abuse on multiple occasions.

Ankita Rao, "Social Media Companies Are Not Free Speech Platforms," Motherboard, November 25, 2016. https://motherboard.vice.com.

is not. It will categorize some fake news articles as legitimate, and more importantly, it will also classify some legitimate news items as fraudulent. As a free-speech advocacy group points out, mistakes such as these "would have severe repercussions on the visibility and findability of news on the platform, and therefore the reach of numerous media outlets."[57] An attempt to suppress fake news, with the best of intentions, could easily interfere with other people's ability to get their message across.

Moreover, defining fake news can be very difficult. "What about erroneous or unverified information that doesn't necessarily intend to deceive but is false all the same?" asks journalist Attila Mong. "Sloppy journalism can have an enormous impact. But is it fake news?"[58]

> "Sloppy journalism can have an enormous impact. But is it fake news?"[58]
>
> —Journalist Attila Mong

The same question applies to satire. Satiric publications such as the *Onion* stay in business by running headlines such as "Follow-Up Tests Confirm President Trump's 19 Other Personalities Also Perfectly Healthy."[59] These headlines are jokes and not intended to be taken seriously. But it can be difficult to recognize whether an article is an example of fake news designed to fool people or a satiric item meant to amuse. The chance that a crackdown on fake news might also eliminate satire and other forms of expression concerns many free-speech advocates.

Harassment and Abuse

While companies like Twitter were hard at work trying to decide what to do about fake news, another controversy about speech on the Internet began to unfold. This one dealt with the prevalence of offensive speech on the Internet. To a large degree, this was not a new problem. Cyberbullying, in which groups of high school or middle school students send cruel or offensive texts, e-mails, and instant messages to a victim, has been going on for years. Women have often complained of poor treatment on certain Internet sites, especially those having to do with gaming. Many have had to put up with suggestive language, personal insults, and threats of physical violence. The culture of the Internet generally allowed comments like these to stand, usually without penalty to the person making them.

In the mid-2010s, though, opinion on this subject began to change as those victimized by online harassment became more willing to fight back. One of their first targets was an app called

Yik Yak, which allowed users to post information, jokes, and other material anonymously. Originally intended for use by college students, Yik Yak functioned as a message board where users could complain about assignments, report lost items, or inform fellow students about goings-on on campus. Many students appreciated the information Yik Yak provided and enjoyed the online conversations sparked by postings. Yik Yak "formed a lot of camaraderie between students,"[60] says a student at a Massachusetts university.

But at many colleges, racist and sexist posts quickly began to appear on Yik Yak. Notices about upcoming concerts and lectures were lost in a deluge of obscene language and sexual references. Cyberbullies singled out students for a steady stream of abuse. In 2015 seven students at the College of Idaho told the school's administration that they were being harassed via the app. The college listened to the students and agreed that their complaints were valid. Part of the issue, administrators noted, was the anonymity of the site. "If someone puts a racist epithet on a Latino's door, or a black person's door," said College of Idaho president Marv Henberg, "there's at least a potential evidence thread that can be investigated. Not with Yik Yak."[61] In the end, the college banned Yik Yak from the campus.

First Amendment Issues

Yik Yak caused similar problems elsewhere as well. At the University of Mary Washington in Virginia, feminist students were targeted in an organized campaign of harassment. When they demanded that college officials ban Yik Yak from the campus, however, administrators refused, citing First Amendment issues. Other commentators agreed that banning Yik Yak raised concerns about free speech. "What's at stake here is the broader principle of expression,"[62] said an ACLU official. An editorial in the online magazine *Slate* pointed out that offensive speech was not limited to the Internet, let alone to Yik Yak: "If we banned every network where harassment and abuse occurs," the editorial argued, "we'd have to get rid of . . . city streets, private homes, churches, and college campuses themselves."[63]

Use of Yik Yak declined precipitously beginning in 2015. The app shut down altogether in 2017, the victim of several high-profile bannings from colleges and plenty of negative publicity. By then, activists had turned their attention to harassment on other social media sites. They demanded that the companies police their users more thoroughly, banning those whose posts were offensive. The companies listened. In 2015 a right-wing Twitter user named Chuck Johnson sent out an appeal for funds from his followers. He said he wanted the money to help him kill DeRay Mckesson, a Black Lives Matter activist. Twitter responded by banning Johnson altogether. In 2016, similarly, Milo Yiannopoulos posted a series of racist and sexist tweets aimed at African American actor Leslie Jones. Like Johnson, Yiannopoulos was given a permanent ban.

Charlottesville

But social media sites did not begin monitoring the speech of users in earnest until late 2017. That August, white supremacists and neo-Nazis gathered in Charlottesville, Virginia, for a Unite the Right rally. The rally, which took place over two days, attracted several hundred white nationalists and more than twice that many protesting the rally. The groups were supposed to remain separate but did not. Violence soon broke out. Several dozen people were injured, and one protester, Heather Heyer, was killed when a white supremacist drove his car into a crowd. The event horrified millions of Americans, both because of the ugliness of the rally—participants shouted Nazi slogans and hurled insults at Jews, Muslims, and African Americans—and because of Heyer's death.

It quickly became clear that the neo-Nazis had used social media sites to plan the rally. The Facebook pages of many of the attendees, moreover, included threats of violence against Jews and racial minorities. Appalled and perhaps embarrassed, Zuckerberg promised that Facebook would immediately take down threats of violence. He also threatened to ban users who engaged in hate speech. "There is no place for hate in our community,"[64] he said. In the next few days, Facebook did indeed delete a number of accounts belonging to white supremacists and neo-Nazi organizations, including the one belonging to rally organizer Christopher Cantwell.

> ## "There is no place for hate in our community."[64]
>
> —Facebook cofounder Mark Zuckerberg

Other Internet sites joined in. When the Southern Poverty Law Center (a legal advocacy organization specializing in civil rights and public interest litigation) reported that white supremacists had used the financial platform PayPal to raise funds for the Charlottesville rally, PayPal announced that it would refuse to "accept payments or donations for activities that promote hate,

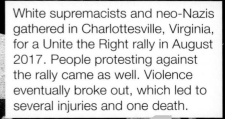

White supremacists and neo-Nazis gathered in Charlottesville, Virginia, for a Unite the Right rally in August 2017. People protesting against the rally came as well. Violence eventually broke out, which led to several injuries and one death.

violence or racial intolerance."[65] The company promptly banned the accounts associated with several prominent white nationalists and neo-Nazi groups. Video-sharing website YouTube did the same, hoping to prevent the supremacists from using its platform to spread their message. The music subscription service Spotify, similarly, announced that it would no longer allow users to listen to music that advocated white power. With one Internet site after another being closed to them, the far right seemed to have suffered a major blow to its cause.

Infringement of Speech?

Some people, however, were not happy with the actions of these companies following Charlottesville. Several whose accounts had been suspended argued that their right to free speech had been violated. "Twitter is censoring right-leaning accounts and suppressing the views of those they don't like," complained Johnson. "They claim that its users have freedom of speech, but it's fraudulent."[66] From a legal perspective, Johnson was wrong; Twitter, Facebook, and other such sites are privately owned, so they are not held to the same standard as a government would be where speech is concerned. Still, Johnson was correct that banning far-right voices had the effect of limiting discourse online, and even some civil liberties activists share his perception that political bias led to the bannings.

> "Twitter is censoring right-leaning accounts and suppressing the views of those they don't like."[66]
>
> —Right-wing Twitter user Chuck Johnson

Indeed, Johnson's views on censorship are shared by many observers who bitterly oppose the far right's agenda. They believe that Johnson's words were offensive, but they also agree that blocking his offensive speech from Facebook or Twitter is a blow against free expression. When unpopular speech is deleted from social media, these commentators point out, the site can become an echo chamber, in which only a narrow range of viewpoints can be expressed. That does not live up to the ideal of former Supreme Court justice William Brennan, who wrote approvingly of "the principle that debate on public issues should be uninhibited, robust, and wide-open."[67] Moreover, it ignores the idea that even objectionable speech must be protected—an idea that has long been a foundation of the right to speak freely.

Free-speech advocates also worry that censorship of white supremacists may turn out to be only the beginning. Many forms of speech can be construed as racist—or sexist, ageist, or otherwise discriminatory and offensive. Should they all be banned, and if not, activists ask, why not? "Now that Spotify has laid out criteria for what music is offensive enough to be removed," writes commentator Amy X. Wang, "will it apply the same standards to all songs in the future? Who will judge?"[68] For that matter, many books, movies, and songs of the past include elements offensive to minorities, women, gays, the disabled, and more. She wonders if they are to be banned, too. It is possible to imagine a time when all that is permitted on the Internet is material that is offensive to no one; it is hard to see that Internet as a compelling place to visit.

> "Now that Spotify has laid out criteria for what music is offensive enough to be removed, will it apply the same standards to all songs in the future? Who will judge?"[68]
>
> —Writer Amy X. Wang

Even if sites like Facebook do not have the powers of government, some observers argue that freedom of speech on the Internet is of great importance to the health of the country. The reason is the massive popularity of Twitter, Facebook, and other similar sites. An enormous number of people get much of their news and other information from tweets and from articles recommended by Facebook friends. Anyone who wants his or her ideas to influence others would be well advised, then, to establish a social media presence. People do have the right to speak freely, but that may be of little use if the best methods for communicating their ideas are off limits to them. "Social platforms . . . aren't bound by the First Amendment," notes journalist Alex Kantrowitz. "But their decisions matter since much of the political discussion that once took place in the open web is now occurring within their walls. . . . Limiting someone's ability to message on Twitter therefore has real impact."[69]

The Internet provides a fascinating example of the tension between free speech and what might seem to be the public good. Few Americans would argue that fake news adds value to the world. In fact, given the potential dangers it creates, there are strong justifications for limiting it or even trying to eradicate it. Most Americans, likewise, would say that there is no room for hate speech in society, and many would support, even applaud, the removal of offensive posts, obscene messages, and threatening tweets from the Internet. At the same time, though, it is important to remember that free speech suffers when companies like Facebook and Twitter begin monitoring the activities of their users—even or perhaps especially when they are pushed to do so, as most observers agree they are, by the public and by politicians. Whether the risks of restricting speech outweigh the benefits of controlling the excesses of open discourse remains to be seen.

SOURCE NOTES

Introduction: Free Speech

1. Laurel Lancaster, "Free Speech Is a Right, Not an Excuse," Odyssey, April 18, 2017. www.theodysseyonline.com.
2. Quoted in Geoffrey R. Stone and Eugene Volokh, "A Common Interpretation: Freedom of Speech and the Press," *Constitution Daily* (blog), National Constitution Center, December 1, 2016. https://constitutioncenter.org.
3. Quoted in Jonathan Israel, *The Expanding Blaze*. Princeton, NJ: Princeton University Press, 2017, p. 352.
4. Quoted in Eric P. Robinson, "During World War I, a Silent Film Spoke Volumes About Free Speech," The Conversation, April 6, 2017. https://theconversation.com.
5. Quoted in Cleve R. Wootsen Jr., "Obama Should Be Arrested for Implying Trump Needs a Filter, Fox Business Host Suggests," *Washington Post*, December 2, 2017. www.washingtonpost.com.

Chapter 1: Unprotected Speech

6. Emily Doskow, "Defamation Law Made Simple," *Nolo*, 2018. www.nolo.com.
7. Quoted in John Murawski, "Wake Jury Awards $7.5 Million to Punish N&O in Libel Trial," *Raleigh (NC) News & Observer*, October 19, 2016. www.newsobserver.com.
8. Quoted in Newseum Institute, "Incitement to Imminent Lawless Action," May 12, 2008. www.newseuminstitute.org.
9. *Brandenburg v. Ohio*, 395 U.S. 444 (1969).
10. Quoted in Michael Edward Lenert, *The Free Flow of Information*. Morrisville, NC: Lulu, 2014, p. 103.
11. Mark Theoharis, "Criminal Threats," Criminal Defense Lawyer, 2018. www.criminaldefenselawyer.com.
12. Quoted in Jason Trahan, "43-Year-Old Northeast Dallas Man Sentenced to More than Two Years in Federal Pris-

on for Posting Threat to Kill Obama Online," *Dallas Morning News*, November 1, 2010. www.dallasnews.com.

13. Quoted in Jillian C. York, "These Days, It's Facebook That Defines Pornography," *Chicago Tribune*, May 30, 2016. www.chicagotribune.com.

14. Kevin Draper, "ESPN Fires Curt Schilling, Who Finally Became Too Much of an Embarrassment," Deadspin, April 20, 2016. https://deadspin.com.

15. Quoted in Keri Blakinger, "ESPN's Curt Schilling Says Hillary Clinton Should Be 'Buried Under a Jail,'" *New York Daily News*, March 2, 2016. www.nydailynews.com.

16. Quoted in Richard Sandomir, "Curt Schilling, ESPN Analyst, Is Fired over Social Media Post," *New York Times*, April 20, 2016. www.nytimes.com.

17. *York (PA) Dispatch*, "Freedom of Speech Comes with Consequences," April 27, 2016. www.yorkdispatch.com.

18. Fredrik deBoer, "Corporations Are Cracking Down on Free Speech Inside the Office—and Out," *Washington Post*, August 11, 2017. www.washingtonpost.com.

Chapter 2: Free Speech on Campus

19. Quoted in Charles Snow, "Why the University Must Be a 'Marketplace of Ideas,'" Alliance Defending Freedom, October 19, 2017. www.adflegal.org.

20. Snow, "Why the University Must Be a 'Marketplace of Ideas.'"

21. Quoted in Jeremy Bauer-Wolf, "The Death of College Free-Speech Zones," *Inside Higher Ed*, February 2, 2018. www.insidehighered.com.

22. Quoted in Alliance Defending Freedom, "'Speech Zones' and 'Speech Codes' Struck Down at Texas Tech University," October 1, 2004. https://adflegal.org.

23. Adam Goldstein, "Kentucky's Controversial 'Charlie Brown' Bill Has Two Provisions Worth Celebrating," FIRE, March 21, 2017. www.thefire.org.

24. Quoted in Erwin Chemerinsky, interviewed by Natalie Shutler, "The Free Speech–Hate Speech Trade-Off," *New York Times*, September 13, 2017. www.nytimes.com.

25. Reed E. McDonnell, "Why Harvard's Hate Speech Policies Are Necessary," *Harvard Crimson*, April 18, 2012. www.thecrimson.com.

26. Quoted in Harrison Aronoff, "College Receives 'Red Light' Free Speech Rating," *Dartmouth*, February 2, 2018. www.thedartmouth.com.
27. Quoted in Chemerinksy, interviewed by Shutler, "The Free Speech–Hate Speech Trade-Off."
28. Quoted in Ideas Desk, "University of Chicago: 'We Do Not Support So-Called Trigger Warnings,'" *Time*, August 25, 2016. http://time.com.
29. Quoted in Thomas Fuller, "Conservative Groups Sue Berkeley over Ann Coulter Cancellation," *New York Times*, April 24, 2017. www.nytimes.com.
30. Quoted in Fuller, "Conservative Groups Sue Berkeley over Ann Coulter Cancellation."
31. Quoted in Chris McGreal, "John Derbyshire Fired for Article Urging Children to Avoid African Americans," *Guardian* (Manchester), April 8, 2012. www.theguardian.com.
32. Quoted in Eric Levenson, "Protestors Heckle Richard Spencer at Univ. of Florida Talk," CNN, October 19, 2017. www.cnn.com.
33. Quoted in Lukas Mikelionis, "Black Lives Matter Shouts Down ACLU: 'You Protect Hitler, Too!,'" Fox News, October 5, 2017. www.foxnews.com.
34. Quoted in Francesca Truitt, "Black Lives Matter Protests American Civil Liberties Union," *Flat Hat* (College of William & Mary), October 2, 2017. http://flathatnews.com.
35. Quoted in Levenson, "Protestors Heckle Richard Spencer at Univ. of Florida Talk."
36. Lili Carneglia, "Keep Fighting Anti-free Speech Activism," *Crimson White* (University of Alabama), October 17, 2016. www.cw.ua.edu.

Chapter 3: Artistic Expression

37. Quoted in Alison Flood, "*Curious Incident of the Dog in the Night-Time* Pulled from Children's Reading Lists," *Guardian* (Manchester), August 12, 2015. www.theguardian.com.
38. Quoted in Erin Adler, "Burnsville's Ames Center Drops Play by Biracial Writer over Use of Word 'Mulatto' in Title," *Minneapolis Star Tribune*, April 19, 2017. www.startribune.com.

39. Quoted in Frank Lombardi, "Christine Quinn Rips 'Horrifying' Game Rapelay," *New York Daily News*, February 24, 2009. www.nydailynews.com.
40. Quoted in David K. Shipler, *Freedom of Speech*. New York: Knopf, 2015, p. 56.
41. Quoted in Lorena Munoz-Alonso, "Dana Schutz's Painting of Emmett Till at Whitney Biennial Sparks Protest," Artnet News, March 21, 2017. https://news.artnet.com.
42. Quoted in Jonathan Jones, "Arguing over Art Is Right but Trying to Ban It Is the Work of Fascists," *Guardian* (Manchester), December 7, 2017. www.theguardian.com.
43. Quoted in Jim Avila et al., "School Shooter: 'I Didn't Realize' They Would Die," ABC News, June 11, 2008. http://abcnews.go.com.
44. Julie Trébault, "Protecting Artists Is More Important Now than Ever," *Huffington Post*, October 11, 2017. www.huffingtonpost.com.
45. Quoted in Priscilla Frank, "A Brief History of Art Censorship from 1508 to 2014," *Huffington Post*, January 16, 2015. www.huffingtonpost.com.
46. Richard L. Lewis and Susan Ingalls Lewis, *The Power of Art*, 3rd ed. Boston: Cengage Learning, 2013, p. 122.
47. ACLU, "What Is Censorship?," 2018. www.aclu.org.
48. Quoted in Agata Blaszczak-Boxe, "Questioning the Role of Media Violence in Violent Acts," CBS News, November 5, 2014. www.cbsnews.com.
49. Quoted in Shipler, *Freedom of Speech*, p. 57.
50. Quoted in Robert P. Doyle, "2015–2016 Books Challenged or Banned," Illinois Library Association, 2016. www.ila.org.
51. Quoted in Claire Mullally and Andrew Gargano, "Banned Books," Newseum Institute, November 29, 2017. www.newseuminstitute.org.
52. ACLU, "Freedom of Expression in the Arts and Entertainment," 2018. www.aclu.org.

Chapter 4: Free Speech and the Internet

53. Steven Levy, "The Internet Isn't the Wild Wild West Anymore. It's Westworld," *Wired*, April 1, 2017. www.wired.com.

54. Quoted in Craig Silverman, "How the Bizarre Conspiracy Theory Behind 'Pizzagate' Was Spread," BuzzFeed, November 4, 2016. www.buzzfeed.com.

55. Quoted in Tony Romm and Kurt Wagner, "Facebook Admits 'Malicious Actors' Spread Misinformation During the 2016 U.S. Election," Recode, April 28, 2017. www.recode.net.

56. Quoted in Jordan Crook, "Fake Times," TechCrunch, March 19, 2017. https://techcrunch.com.

57. Article 19, "Free Speech Concerns Amid the 'Fake News' Fad," January 18, 2018. www.article19.org.

58. Attila Mong, "Countering Fake News While Safeguarding Free Speech," DW Akademie, March 14, 2017. www.dw.com.

59. *Onion*, "Follow-Up Tests Confirm President Trump's 19 Other Personalities Also Perfectly Healthy," January 17, 2018. https://politics.theonion.com.

60. Quoted in Valeriya Safronova, "The Rise and Fall of Yik Yak, the Anonymous Messaging App," *New York Times*, May 27, 2017. www.nytimes.com.

61. Quoted in Hannah Orenstein, "Colleges Are Starting to Ban Yik Yak on Campus," *Cosmopolitan*, May 15, 2016. www.cosmopolitan.com.

62. Quoted in Orenstein, "Colleges Are Starting to Ban Yik Yak on Campus."

63. Amanda Hess, "Don't Ban Yik Yak," *Slate*, October 28, 2015. www.slate.com.

64. Quoted in Julia Carrie Wong, "Mark Zuckerberg on Charlottesville: Facebook Will Remove Violent Threats," *Guardian* (Manchester), August 16, 2017. www.theguardian.com.

65. Quoted in Wong, "Mark Zuckerberg on Charlottesville."

66. Quoted in Terry Collins, "'Alt-right' Activist Chuck Johnson Sues Twitter for Banning Him," CNET, January 9, 2018. www.cnet.com.

67. Quoted in Lincoln Caplan, "Should Facebook and Twitter Be Regulated Under the First Amendment?," *Wired*, October 11, 2017. www.wired.com.

68. Quoted in Andy Hermann, "Fine, Let's Talk About White Supremacist Hate Bands," *LA Weekly*, August 19, 2017. www.laweekly.com.

69. Alex Kantrowitz, "Twitter Unverifies Writer Amid Speech Wars," BuzzFeed, January 9, 2016. www.buzzfeed.com.

Alliance Defending Freedom
15100 N. Ninetieth St.
Scottsdale, AZ 85260
website: www.adflegal.org

This organization concerns itself with religious liberty and approaches public policy issues from a politically conservative point of view. It takes a particular interest in helping college students who believe that their right to free speech is being denied, whether because they express conservative views or because others are not comfortable with overtly Christian speech.

American Civil Liberties Union (ACLU)
125 Broad St., Eighteenth Floor
New York, NY 10004
website: www.aclu.org

The ACLU promotes and defends the civil liberties enumerated in the Bill of Rights. It is known especially for its strong support of freedom of speech, even from people who express unpopular or potentially dangerous perspectives. It provides position papers, policy statements, and other materials relating to free speech and other civil rights.

American Library Association (ALA)
50 E. Huron St.
Chicago, IL 60611
website: www.ala.org

The ALA was the world's first association of librarians; today it is also the biggest. In addition to supporting librarians in their careers and advocating library funding, the ALA also takes an interest in free-speech rights by opposing the banning of books from public libraries and school libraries, along with opposing the removal of controversial reading matter from the K–12 curriculum.

First Amendment Coalition
534 Fourth St., Suite B
San Rafael, CA 94901
website: https://firstamendmentcoalition.org

This is an advocacy group that educates the public about free speech and related issues, notably freedom of the press and openness in government. The coalition offers legal help to journalists, academics, and other people who believe their free-speech rights are being restricted. It also provides workshops, educational materials, and other programs to inform people of their rights.

Foundation for Individual Rights in Education (FIRE)
website: www.thefire.org

FIRE focuses on the rights of college and graduate students and professors at American universities. One of its main goals is to defend freedom of speech where it is threatened by college administrators and others. Though it is a nonpartisan organization, it most often supports Christian and conservative students and student groups whose speech rights have been threatened.

Newseum Institute
website: www.newseuminstitute.org

The Newseum is a museum in Washington, DC, that focuses on the media in America. The Newseum Institute is an arm of the museum that educates people about First Amendment issues, including freedom of speech. The institute's offerings include articles, podcasts, and other information about the First Amendment in history and in modern times.

FOR FURTHER RESEARCH

Books

Floyd Abrams, *The Soul of the First Amendment*. New Haven, CT: Yale University Press, 2018.

Erwin Chemerinsky and Howard Gillman, *Free Speech on Campus*. New Haven, CT: Yale University Press, 2017.

Stephen Currie, *Sharing Posts: The Spread of Fake News*. San Diego: ReferencePoint, 2018.

David K. Shipler, *Freedom of Speech*. New York: Knopf, 2015.

Mark V. Tushnet, Alan Chen, and Joseph Blocher, *Free Speech Beyond Words: The Surprising Reach of the First Amendment*. New York: New York University Press, 2017.

Internet Sources

Erwin Chemerinsky, interviewed by Natalie Shutler, "The Free Speech–Hate Speech Trade-Off," On Campus *New York Times*, September 13, 2017. www.nytimes.com/2017/09/13 /opinion/berkeley-dean-erwin-chemerinsky.html.

Jonathan Jones, "Arguing over Art Is Right but Trying to Ban It Is the Work of Fascists," *Guardian* (Manchester), December 7, 2017. www.theguardian.com/artanddesign/2017/dec /07/arguing-over-art-is-right-but-trying-to-ban-it-is-the-work -of-fascists.

Valeriya Safronova, "The Rise and Fall of Yik Yak, the Anonymous Messaging App," *New York Times*, May 27, 2017. www.nytimes.com/2017/05/27/style/yik-yak-bullying-mary -washington.html.

Charles Snow, "Why the University Must Be a 'Marketplace of Ideas,'" Alliance Defending Freedom, October 19, 2017.

www.adflegal.org/detailspages/blog-details/allianceedge
/2017/10/19/why-the-university-must-be-a-marketplace-of
-ideas.

Geoffrey R. Stone and Eugene Volokh, "A Common Interpretation: Freedom of Speech and the Press," *Constitution Daily* (blog),
National Constitution Center, December 1, 2016. https://con
stitutioncenter.org/blog/a-common-interpretation-freedom-of
-speech-and-the-press.

US Constitution, National Archives, 2017. www.archives.gov
/founding-docs/constitution-transcript.

INDEX

Note: Boldface page numbers indicate illustrations.

PICTURE CREDITS

Stephen Currie has written many books for young adults and children. His works for ReferencePoint Press includes *Sharing Posts: The Spread of Fake News*; *Thinking Critically: Cyberbullying*; *Forgotten Youth: Undocumented Immigrant Youth*; *Teen Guide to Finance: Teen Guide to Saving and Investing*; *Cause & Effect: The Ancient Maya*; and *Issues in the Digital Age: Online Privacy*. He has also taught grade levels ranging from kindergarten to college. He lives in New York's Hudson Valley.